My Grimoire of Spells Incantations Hexes Curses Divinations and other Witchcraft

Property of the Enchanting

Witch, Sorcerer, Magic Wielder

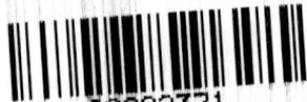

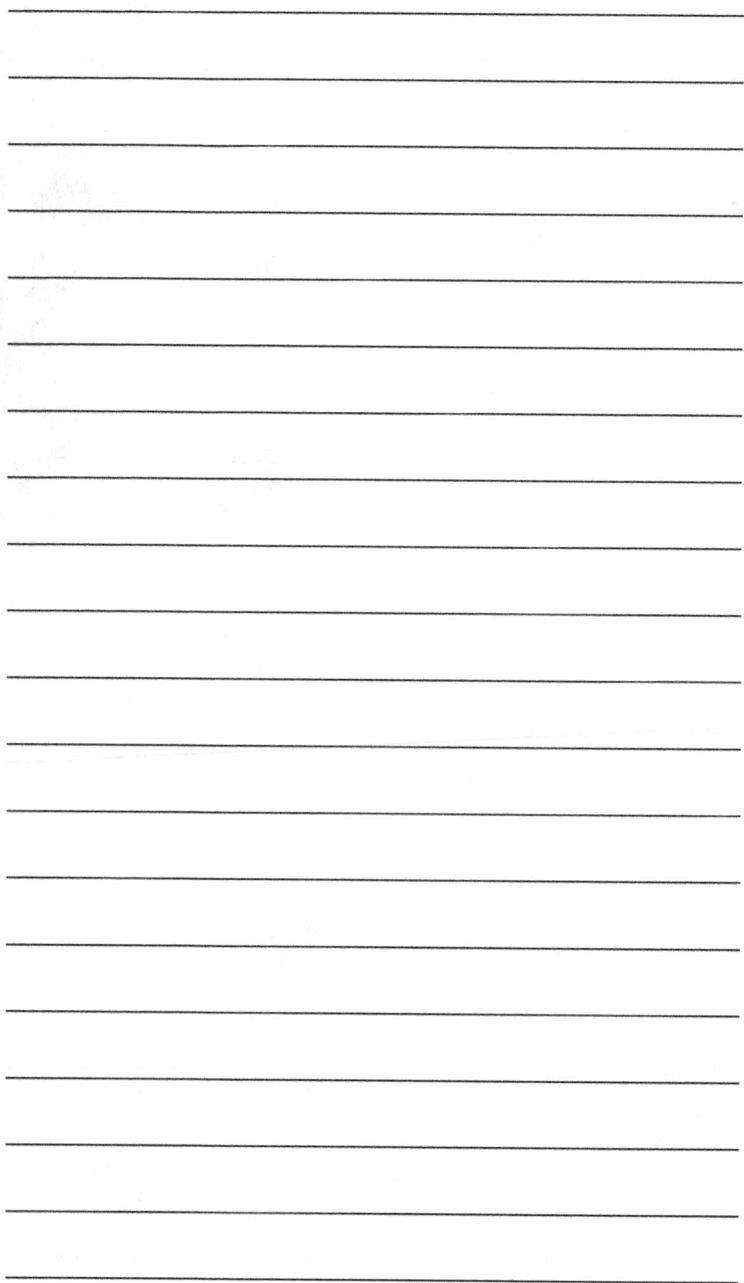

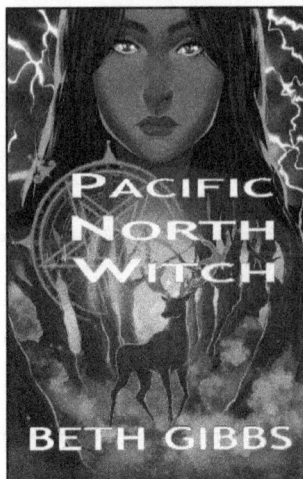

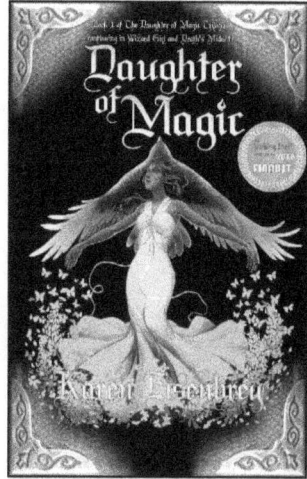